EMMANUEL JOSEPH

The Nexus of Vitality, Integrating Wellness, Wealth, and Personal Renaissance

Copyright © 2025 by Emmanuel Joseph

All rights reserved. No part of this publication may be reproduced, stored or transmitted in any form or by any means, electronic, mechanical, photocopying, recording, scanning, or otherwise without written permission from the publisher. It is illegal to copy this book, post it to a website, or distribute it by any other means without permission.

First edition

*This book was professionally typeset on Reedsy.
Find out more at reedsy.com*

Contents

1. Chapter 1: Awakening to a New Reality — 1
2. Chapter 2: The Power of Financial Freedom — 3
3. Chapter 3: Embracing Mindfulness and Meditation — 5
4. Chapter 4: Cultivating Emotional Intelligence — 7
5. Chapter 5: The Art of Goal Setting — 9
6. Chapter 6: Nurturing Relationships — 11
7. Chapter 7: The Importance of Lifelong Learning — 13
8. Chapter 8: The Role of Creativity in Personal Growth — 15
9. Chapter 9: The Power of Positive Thinking — 17
10. Chapter 10: The Art of Self-Care — 19
11. Chapter 11: The Impact of Physical Activity — 21
12. Chapter 12: The Power of Nutrition — 23
13. Chapter 13: The Role of Sleep in Overall Health — 25
14. Chapter 14: The Importance of Community and Connection — 27
15. Chapter 15: The Journey Towards Personal Renaissance — 29

1

Chapter 1: Awakening to a New Reality

The dawn of a new era is upon us—a time where wellness, wealth, and personal renaissance merge to form a powerful nexus of vitality. This transformation begins with a shift in consciousness, an awakening to the interconnectedness of our physical, mental, and emotional well-being. As we embark on this journey, we must first acknowledge the importance of balance and harmony in our lives. By embracing a holistic approach, we can unlock the true potential that lies within us, paving the way for a life of abundance and fulfillment.

To achieve this, we must cultivate a mindset of growth and self-discovery. This involves shedding limiting beliefs and embracing the limitless possibilities that life has to offer. By developing a strong foundation of self-awareness, we can better understand our strengths, weaknesses, and unique gifts. This self-knowledge empowers us to make conscious choices that align with our core values and aspirations, ultimately leading to a more purposeful and meaningful existence.

As we delve deeper into this new reality, we must also recognize the importance of nurturing our physical health. Our bodies are the vessels through which we experience life, and by prioritizing our well-being, we can enhance our overall quality of life. This includes adopting healthy habits such as regular exercise, balanced nutrition, and adequate rest. By honoring our bodies and treating them with respect, we can create a solid foundation upon which to build our personal renaissance.

In addition to physical health, mental and emotional well-being are equally crucial components of the nexus of vitality. By cultivating a positive mindset and practicing mindfulness, we can develop resilience and inner peace. This allows us to navigate life's challenges with grace and clarity, ultimately leading to greater happiness and fulfillment. As we continue on this journey, we must remember that true wellness is a lifelong pursuit—one that requires consistent effort, dedication, and self-compassion.

2

Chapter 2: The Power of Financial Freedom

Financial freedom is a critical aspect of the nexus of vitality, as it provides the means to pursue our passions and live a life of abundance. Achieving financial independence requires a combination of strategic planning, disciplined saving, and smart investing. By taking control of our finances, we can create a stable foundation that supports our personal growth and well-being.

The first step towards financial freedom is developing a clear understanding of our financial situation. This involves assessing our income, expenses, debts, and assets. By creating a comprehensive budget, we can identify areas where we can cut back on unnecessary spending and allocate funds towards our financial goals. This process requires discipline and commitment, but the rewards are well worth the effort.

In addition to budgeting, it is essential to develop a long-term financial plan that includes saving for retirement, building an emergency fund, and investing in assets that generate passive income. By diversifying our investments and minimizing risk, we can create a steady stream of income that supports our desired lifestyle. This financial stability allows us to focus on our personal renaissance and pursue activities that bring us joy and fulfillment.

Another important aspect of financial freedom is developing a healthy relationship with money. This involves shifting our mindset from scarcity to abundance and recognizing that wealth is a tool that can be used to create positive change in our lives and the lives of others. By cultivating an attitude of gratitude and generosity, we can attract more abundance into our lives and use our wealth to make a meaningful impact on the world.

3

Chapter 3: Embracing Mindfulness and Meditation

Mindfulness and meditation are powerful practices that can help us achieve a state of inner peace and clarity. By focusing our attention on the present moment, we can cultivate a deeper awareness of our thoughts, emotions, and physical sensations. This heightened awareness allows us to better understand ourselves and make conscious choices that align with our true desires and aspirations.

The practice of mindfulness involves paying attention to our thoughts and feelings without judgment. By observing our inner experiences with curiosity and compassion, we can develop a greater understanding of our mental and emotional patterns. This self-awareness empowers us to respond to life's challenges with greater resilience and equanimity, ultimately leading to a more balanced and fulfilling life.

Meditation is a complementary practice that can help us cultivate mindfulness and deepen our connection to our inner selves. By setting aside time each day to sit quietly and focus on our breath, we can quiet the mind and access a state of inner stillness. This practice allows us to release stress and tension, promoting a sense of calm and relaxation that benefits both our mental and physical health.

Incorporating mindfulness and meditation into our daily routine can have profound effects on our overall well-being. By developing a regular practice, we can cultivate a greater sense of presence and inner peace, which in turn enhances our ability to navigate life's challenges with grace and clarity. As we continue on our journey of personal renaissance, these practices serve as essential tools for achieving a state of holistic wellness.

4

Chapter 4: Cultivating Emotional Intelligence

Emotional intelligence is a key component of the nexus of vitality, as it enables us to navigate our relationships and interactions with greater ease and understanding. By developing our emotional intelligence, we can enhance our ability to communicate effectively, manage stress, and build meaningful connections with others.

The first step in cultivating emotional intelligence is developing self-awareness. This involves recognizing and understanding our own emotions, as well as the impact they have on our thoughts and behaviors. By paying attention to our emotional responses, we can gain valuable insights into our underlying needs and desires, ultimately leading to greater self-acceptance and personal growth.

In addition to self-awareness, emotional intelligence also involves the ability to regulate our emotions. This means managing our emotional responses in a healthy and constructive manner, rather than allowing them to control our actions. By developing strategies for coping with stress and negative emotions, we can maintain a sense of balance and inner peace, even in challenging situations.

Another important aspect of emotional intelligence is empathy, or the ability to understand and share the feelings of others. By cultivating empathy, we can build stronger, more compassionate relationships and foster a sense of connection and belonging. This involves actively listening to others, validating their emotions, and responding with kindness and understanding.

As we continue to develop our emotional intelligence, we can enhance our overall well-being and create a more harmonious and fulfilling life. By cultivating self-awareness, emotional regulation, and empathy, we can navigate our relationships and interactions with greater ease and understanding, ultimately contributing to our personal renaissance and the nexus of vitality.

5

Chapter 5: The Art of Goal Setting

Goal setting is a powerful tool for achieving success and fulfillment in all areas of life. By setting clear, achievable goals, we can create a roadmap for our personal and professional growth, ultimately leading to a more purposeful and meaningful existence.

The first step in effective goal setting is identifying our core values and aspirations. By gaining clarity on what truly matters to us, we can set goals that align with our passions and priorities. This process involves introspection and self-reflection, as well as a willingness to explore our deepest desires and dreams.

Once we have identified our core values and aspirations, the next step is to set specific, measurable, and time-bound goals. By breaking our larger aspirations into smaller, manageable steps, we can create a clear path towards achieving our desired outcomes. This involves setting short-term, medium-term, and long-term goals, as well as regularly reviewing and adjusting our progress.

In addition to setting goals, it is essential to develop a plan of action that outlines the steps we need to take to achieve our objectives. This involves prioritizing tasks, allocating resources, and setting deadlines to ensure we stay on track. By creating a detailed action plan, we can maintain focus and motivation, ultimately leading to greater success and fulfillment.

Finally, it is important to celebrate our achievements and recognize the progress we have made. By acknowledging our successes, we can build confidence and reinforce our commitment to our goals. This positive reinforcement helps to create a cycle of continuous growth and improvement, ultimately contributing to our personal renaissance and the nexus of vitality.

6

Chapter 6: Nurturing Relationships

Relationships are a fundamental aspect of the nexus of vitality, as they provide us with support, connection, and a sense of belonging. By nurturing our relationships, we can create a strong network of positive influences that enhance our overall well-being and contribute to our personal growth.

The first step in nurturing relationships is developing effective communication skills. This involves actively listening to others, expressing ourselves clearly and honestly, and being open to feedback. By improving our communication skills, we can build stronger, more authentic connections with the people in our lives.

In addition to communication, it is important to cultivate empathy and understanding in our relationships. This means recognizing and validating the emotions and experiences of others, as well as being willing to compromise and find common ground. By fostering a sense of empathy and understanding, we can create more harmonious and supportive relationships that contribute to our overall well-being.

Another important aspect of nurturing relationships is setting healthy boundaries. This involves recognizing our own needs and limits, as well as respecting the boundaries of others. By establishing clear boundaries, we can create a sense of balance and mutual respect in our relationships, ultimately leading to greater harmony and fulfillment.

Finally, it is essential to invest time and effort into maintaining our relationships. This means regularly checking in with the people in our lives, offering support and encouragement, and celebrating their successes. By nurturing our relationships, we can create a strong network of positive influences that enhance our overall well-being and contribute to our personal renaissance and the nexus of vitality.

7

Chapter 7: The Importance of Lifelong Learning

Lifelong learning is a key component of the nexus of vitality, as it enables us to continuously grow and evolve throughout our lives. By embracing a mindset of curiosity and exploration, we can develop new skills, expand our knowledge, and enhance our overall well-being.

The first step in cultivating a love for lifelong learning is developing a growth mindset. This involves recognizing that our abilities and intelligence are not fixed but can be developed through effort and perseverance. By embracing challenges and viewing failures as opportunities for growth, we can cultivate a mindset that supports continuous learning and self-improvement.

To foster a culture of lifelong learning, it is essential to create an environment that encourages curiosity and exploration. This can be achieved by seeking out new experiences, engaging in diverse activities, and exposing ourselves to different perspectives. By staying open to new ideas and experiences, we can continually expand our knowledge and skills, ultimately enhancing our overall well-being.

In addition to seeking out new experiences, it is important to develop effective learning strategies. This includes setting clear learning goals, breaking complex tasks into manageable steps, and regularly reviewing and reflecting on our progress. By developing a structured approach to learning, we can maximize our potential and achieve greater success in our personal and professional lives.

Finally, it is important to recognize the value of learning from others. This involves seeking out mentors, collaborating with peers, and participating in communities of practice. By engaging with others who share our interests and passions, we can gain valuable insights and support that contribute to our personal growth and development. As we continue to embrace lifelong learning, we can unlock new opportunities and experiences that contribute to our personal renaissance and the nexus of vitality.

8

Chapter 8: The Role of Creativity in Personal Growth

Creativity is a vital component of the nexus of vitality, as it allows us to express ourselves, solve problems, and innovate. By nurturing our creative potential, we can enhance our overall well-being and contribute to our personal and professional growth.

The first step in cultivating creativity is developing a mindset of openness and curiosity. This involves embracing new ideas, experimenting with different approaches, and challenging our assumptions. By fostering a sense of curiosity and exploration, we can unlock our creative potential and discover new ways of thinking and doing.

In addition to cultivating a creative mindset, it is important to create an environment that supports creativity. This can be achieved by setting aside dedicated time and space for creative activities, surrounding ourselves with inspiring materials, and minimizing distractions. By creating a supportive environment, we can nurture our creativity and enhance our ability to generate new ideas and solutions.

Another important aspect of nurturing creativity is developing creative habits. This includes regularly engaging in creative activities, such as writing, drawing, or playing music, as well as seeking out new experiences and perspectives. By making creativity a regular part of our lives, we can continually expand our creative potential and enhance our overall well-being.

Finally, it is important to recognize the value of collaboration in the creative process. This involves seeking out opportunities to work with others, sharing ideas and feedback, and building on each other's strengths. By collaborating with others, we can gain new insights and perspectives that contribute to our creative growth and development. As we continue to nurture our creativity, we can unlock new opportunities and experiences that contribute to our personal renaissance and the nexus of vitality.

9

Chapter 9: The Power of Positive Thinking

Positive thinking is a powerful tool that can enhance our overall well-being and contribute to our personal and professional success. By cultivating a positive mindset, we can improve our mental and emotional health, build resilience, and achieve our goals.

The first step in developing a positive mindset is recognizing and challenging negative thought patterns. This involves becoming aware of our self-talk and identifying any limiting beliefs or negative assumptions that may be holding us back. By challenging these negative thoughts and replacing them with positive affirmations, we can shift our mindset from scarcity to abundance and create a more optimistic outlook on life.

In addition to challenging negative thoughts, it is important to practice gratitude and focus on the positive aspects of our lives. This involves regularly reflecting on the things we are thankful for and celebrating our successes, both big and small. By cultivating an attitude of gratitude, we can attract more positivity into our lives and enhance our overall well-being.

Another important aspect of positive thinking is developing resilience in the face of challenges. This involves viewing setbacks as opportunities for growth and maintaining a sense of optimism and determination, even in difficult situations. By developing resilience, we can navigate life's challenges with greater ease and maintain a positive outlook, ultimately leading to greater happiness and fulfillment.

Finally, it is important to surround ourselves with positive influences. This includes building relationships with supportive and uplifting individuals, seeking out inspiring content, and engaging in activities that bring us joy. By surrounding ourselves with positivity, we can create a supportive environment that nurtures our well-being and contributes to our personal renaissance and the nexus of vitality.

10

Chapter 10: The Art of Self-Care

Self-care is a crucial aspect of the nexus of vitality, as it allows us to recharge, rejuvenate, and maintain our overall well-being. By prioritizing self-care, we can enhance our physical, mental, and emotional health, ultimately leading to a more balanced and fulfilling life.

The first step in practicing self-care is recognizing our needs and making a commitment to prioritize our well-being. This involves setting aside time each day to engage in activities that promote relaxation and rejuvenation, such as exercise, meditation, or spending time in nature. By making self-care a regular part of our routine, we can create a solid foundation for overall well-being.

In addition to setting aside time for self-care, it is important to develop healthy habits that support our physical health. This includes eating a balanced diet, getting regular exercise, and ensuring we get enough sleep. By taking care of our bodies, we can enhance our energy levels, improve our mood, and reduce the risk of illness and disease.

Another important aspect of self-care is nurturing our mental and emotional health. This involves engaging in activities that bring us joy and fulfillment, such as pursuing hobbies, spending time with loved ones, and practicing mindfulness and relaxation techniques. By prioritizing our mental and emotional well-being, we can enhance our overall quality of life and create a sense of inner peace and balance.

Finally, it is important to recognize the value of seeking support when needed. This involves reaching out to friends, family, or professionals for guidance and encouragement, as well as being open to receiving help when we need it. By building a strong support network, we can navigate life's challenges with greater ease and maintain our overall well-being, ultimately contributing to our personal renaissance and the nexus of vitality.

11

Chapter 11: The Impact of Physical Activity

Physical activity is a key component of the nexus of vitality, as it promotes overall health and well-being. By incorporating regular exercise into our daily routine, we can enhance our physical, mental, and emotional health, ultimately leading to a more balanced and fulfilling life.

The first step in developing a regular exercise routine is finding activities that we enjoy and that align with our fitness goals. This may include activities such as walking, running, swimming, yoga, or strength training. By choosing activities that we enjoy, we can make exercise a more enjoyable and sustainable part of our daily routine.

In addition to finding enjoyable activities, it is important to set realistic and achievable fitness goals. This involves setting specific, measurable, and time-bound goals, as well as regularly tracking our progress. By setting clear goals and monitoring our progress, we can stay motivated and committed to our fitness journey.

Another important aspect of regular exercise is incorporating variety into our routine. This involves mixing up our workouts and trying new activities to keep things interesting and prevent boredom. By incorporating variety, we can challenge our bodies in different ways and enhance our overall fitness and well-being.

Finally, it is important to recognize the value of rest and recovery in our fitness journey. This involves allowing our bodies time to rest and recover between workouts, as well as incorporating activities such as stretching and foam rolling to prevent injury and promote flexibility. By prioritizing rest and recovery, we can maintain our overall health and well-being and continue to make progress towards our fitness goals.

12

Chapter 12: The Power of Nutrition

Nutrition is a crucial aspect of the nexus of vitality, as it provides the fuel our bodies need to function optimally. By adopting a balanced and nutritious diet, we can enhance our physical, mental, and emotional health, ultimately leading to a more balanced and fulfilling life.

The first step in adopting a balanced diet is understanding the importance of macronutrients and micronutrients. Macronutrients, such as carbohydrates, proteins, and fats, provide the energy our bodies need to function, while micronutrients, such as vitamins and minerals, support various bodily processes. By ensuring we get a balance of both macronutrients and micronutrients, we can support our overall health and well-being.

In addition to understanding the importance of nutrients, it is important to develop healthy eating habits. This includes eating regular meals, choosing whole and unprocessed foods, and practicing portion control. By developing healthy eating habits, we can maintain a stable energy level, support our immune system, and reduce the risk of chronic diseases.

Another important aspect of nutrition is staying hydrated. This involves drinking enough water throughout the day to support our bodily functions and maintain our overall health. By staying hydrated, we can enhance our energy levels, improve our cognitive function, and support our overall well-being.

Finally, it is important to recognize the value of mindful eating. This involves paying attention to our hunger and fullness cues, savoring our food, and avoiding distractions while eating. By practicing mindful eating, we can develop a healthier relationship with food and enhance our overall well-being, ultimately contributing to our personal renaissance and the nexus of vitality.

13

Chapter 13: The Role of Sleep in Overall Health

Sleep is a vital component of the nexus of vitality, as it allows our bodies and minds to rest, recover, and rejuvenate. By prioritizing quality sleep, we can enhance our physical, mental, and emotional health, ultimately leading to a more balanced and fulfilling life.

The first step in prioritizing quality sleep is understanding the importance of sleep hygiene. This involves creating a sleep-friendly environment, such as keeping our bedroom cool, dark, and quiet, and investing in a comfortable mattress and pillows. By optimizing our sleep environment, we can create the ideal conditions for restful and restorative sleep.

In addition to optimizing our sleep environment, it is important to develop a consistent sleep routine. This involves going to bed and waking up at the same time each day, even on weekends. By establishing a regular sleep schedule, we can regulate our body's internal clock and improve the quality of our sleep.

Another important aspect of sleep hygiene is developing healthy pre-sleep habits. This includes winding down before bed by engaging in relaxing activities such as reading, taking a warm bath, or practicing mindfulness. It is also important to limit exposure to screens and electronic devices before bed, as the blue light emitted can interfere with our body's production of melatonin, a hormone that regulates sleep.

Finally, it is important to recognize the value of getting enough sleep. This involves prioritizing sleep and recognizing its impact on our overall health and well-being. By ensuring we get the recommended 7-9 hours of sleep each night, we can enhance our physical, mental, and emotional health, ultimately contributing to our personal renaissance and the nexus of vitality.

14

Chapter 14: The Importance of Community and Connection

Community and connection are vital components of the nexus of vitality, as they provide us with a sense of belonging, support, and purpose. By building and nurturing strong connections with others, we can enhance our overall well-being and contribute to our personal and collective growth.

The first step in building a strong sense of community is recognizing the importance of social connections. This involves seeking out opportunities to connect with others, such as joining clubs, attending events, or participating in volunteer activities. By actively engaging with our community, we can build meaningful relationships and create a sense of belonging.

In addition to seeking out opportunities to connect with others, it is important to develop effective communication skills. This involves actively listening, expressing ourselves clearly and honestly, and being open to feedback. By improving our communication skills, we can build stronger, more authentic connections with the people in our lives.

Another important aspect of building a strong sense of community is fostering a sense of empathy and understanding. This means recognizing and validating the emotions and experiences of others, as well as being willing to compromise and find common ground. By cultivating empathy and understanding, we can create more harmonious and supportive relationships that contribute to our overall well-being.

Finally, it is important to invest time and effort into maintaining our connections. This means regularly checking in with the people in our lives, offering support and encouragement, and celebrating their successes. By nurturing our relationships, we can create a strong network of positive influences that enhance our overall well-being and contribute to our personal renaissance and the nexus of vitality.

15

Chapter 15: The Journey Towards Personal Renaissance

The journey towards a personal renaissance is a lifelong pursuit of growth, self-discovery, and fulfillment. By embracing the principles of wellness, wealth, and personal development, we can create a balanced and harmonious life that aligns with our true desires and aspirations.

The first step in this journey is cultivating a mindset of growth and self-awareness. This involves shedding limiting beliefs, embracing new possibilities, and developing a strong foundation of self-knowledge. By understanding our strengths, weaknesses, and unique gifts, we can make conscious choices that align with our core values and aspirations.

In addition to cultivating self-awareness, it is important to prioritize our physical, mental, and emotional health. This includes adopting healthy habits, such as regular exercise, balanced nutrition, mindfulness practices, and adequate rest. By honoring our bodies and minds, we can create a solid foundation upon which to build our personal renaissance.

Another important aspect of the journey towards personal renaissance is achieving financial freedom. By taking control of our finances, developing a long-term financial plan, and cultivating a healthy relationship with money, we can create a stable foundation that supports our personal growth and well-being.

Finally, it is important to nurture our relationships and connections with others. By developing effective communication skills, cultivating empathy and understanding, and investing time and effort into maintaining our connections, we can create a strong network of positive influences that enhance our overall well-being.

As we continue on this journey, we must remember that true wellness is a lifelong pursuit—one that requires consistent effort, dedication, and self-compassion. By embracing the principles of wellness, wealth, and personal development, we can create a balanced and harmonious life that aligns with our true desires and aspirations, ultimately leading to our personal renaissance and the nexus of vitality.

The Nexus of Vitality: Integrating Wellness, Wealth, and Personal Renaissance is a transformative guide that explores the interconnectedness of holistic well-being, financial freedom, and personal growth. This book invites readers on a journey of self-discovery and empowerment, revealing the keys to unlocking a life of abundance and fulfillment.

Each chapter delves into essential aspects of creating a balanced and harmonious life, from awakening to a new reality and embracing mindfulness, to the power of financial freedom and the importance of self-care. Readers will uncover practical strategies for developing emotional intelligence, setting and achieving goals, nurturing relationships, and cultivating a growth mindset.

Through engaging and thought-provoking insights, The Nexus of Vitality provides readers with the tools and inspiration needed to embark on their personal renaissance. It encourages the integration of physical, mental, and emotional well-being, alongside the pursuit of financial stability and lifelong learning. Ultimately, this book serves as a comprehensive roadmap for anyone seeking to create a vibrant and purposeful life.

www.ingramcontent.com/pod-product-compliance
Lightning Source LLC
LaVergne TN
LVHW010443070526
838199LV00066B/6174